AGE OF DINOSAURS: **APATOSAURUS**

AGE OF DINOSAURS:

Apatosaurus

SARA GILBERT

CREATIVE EDUCATION

Published by Creative Education
P.O. Box 227, Mankato, Minnesota 56002
Creative Education is an imprint of The Creative Company
www.thecreativecompany.us

Design and production by Blue Design
Art direction by Rita Marshall
Printed by Corporate Graphics in the United States of America

Photographs by 123 RF (123rfaurinko), Bridgeman Art Library
(English School, Neave Parker, Francis Phillipps), Corbis (Louie
Psihoyos, Louie Psihoyos/Science Faction, Underwood &
Underwood, Jim Zuckerman), Getty Images (Jerry Cooke/Time
& Life Pictures, DEA Picture Library), iStockphoto (Steve Geer,
Gilles Glod, Michael Gray, Zoltan Kovacs, Ethan Myerson, Allan
Tooley), Library of Congress, Sarah Yakawonis/Blue Design

Library of Congress Cataloging-in-Publication Data
Gilbert, Sara.
Apatosaurus / by Sara Gilbert.
p. cm. — (Age of dinosaurs)
Summary: An introduction to the life and era of the giant,
long-necked dinosaur known as *Apatosaurus*, starting with
the creature's 1877 discovery and ending with present-day
research topics.
Includes bibliographical references and index.
ISBN 978-1-58341-974-8
1. Apatosaurus—Juvenile literature. I. Title. II. Series.

QE862.S3G538 2010
567.913'8—dc22   2009025536

CPSIA: 120109 P01089

First Edition
9 8 7 6 5 4 3 2 1

CONTENTS

APATOSAURUS TALES

Although scientists know what *Apatosaurus* looked like in terms of its skeleton, much of the dinosaur's appearance is left to the imagination.

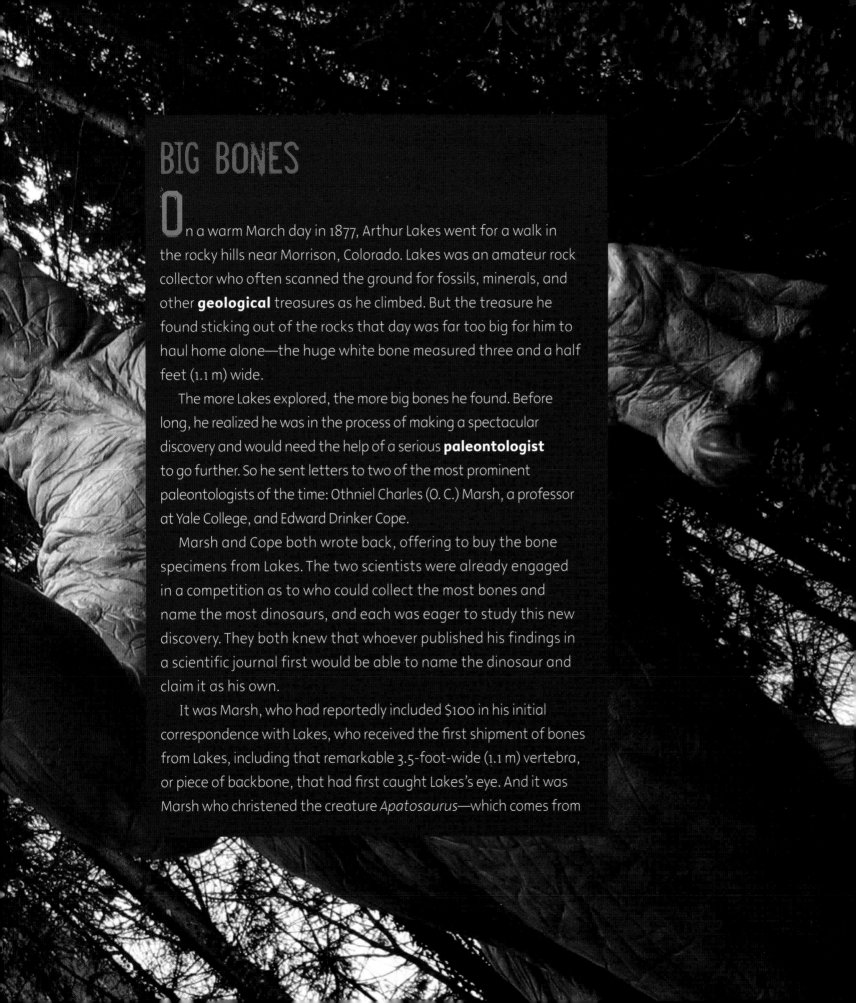

BIG BONES

On a warm March day in 1877, Arthur Lakes went for a walk in the rocky hills near Morrison, Colorado. Lakes was an amateur rock collector who often scanned the ground for fossils, minerals, and other **geological** treasures as he climbed. But the treasure he found sticking out of the rocks that day was far too big for him to haul home alone—the huge white bone measured three and a half feet (1.1 m) wide.

The more Lakes explored, the more big bones he found. Before long, he realized he was in the process of making a spectacular discovery and would need the help of a serious **paleontologist** to go further. So he sent letters to two of the most prominent paleontologists of the time: Othniel Charles (O. C.) Marsh, a professor at Yale College, and Edward Drinker Cope.

Marsh and Cope both wrote back, offering to buy the bone specimens from Lakes. The two scientists were already engaged in a competition as to who could collect the most bones and name the most dinosaurs, and each was eager to study this new discovery. They both knew that whoever published his findings in a scientific journal first would be able to name the dinosaur and claim it as his own.

It was Marsh, who had reportedly included $100 in his initial correspondence with Lakes, who received the first shipment of bones from Lakes, including that remarkable 3.5-foot-wide (1.1 m) vertebra, or piece of backbone, that had first caught Lakes's eye. And it was Marsh who christened the creature *Apatosaurus*—which comes from

Greek words meaning "deceptive lizard"—and categorized it as belonging to the family Diplodocidae.

Although that *Apatosaurus* specimen was far from complete—Lakes had been able to send only pieces of the backbone and a sacrum, or a triangular bone made of two fused vertebrae that is located between the hipbones—it was still considered a major find. The bones were among the largest that had been unearthed to date. Even as Marsh was studying the fossils in his Connecticut lab, dozens of bone hunters were descending upon the previously unsearched hills of central Colorado, hoping to find bigger and better specimens. Not wanting to miss out on the opportunity, both Marsh and Cope dispatched their own men out West with instructions to send back any bones of interest discovered in the area.

The fossil-finding frenzy created by *Apatosaurus* led to the discovery of several other dinosaurs in the same region that year, including *Camarasaurus*, a 59-foot-long (18 m) skeleton whose discovery was claimed by Cope. *Stegosaurus*, a beast whose back was lined with pointed plates, also came out of a Colorado quarry in 1877.

Marsh made several astute observations in his studies of the first *Apatosaurus* bones. He guessed accurately that the dinosaur was a sauropod—a class of large, **herbivorous**, long-necked dinosaurs with small heads and long tails. Because of where *Apatosaurus* had been found and the **sediment** in which it

10

A Man on a Mission

Othniel Charles (O. C.) Marsh grew up on a farm near Lockport, New York, in the 1830s. He dreaded his farm chores and had little appreciation for the bounty of the land—that is, until he met an amateur geologist who opened his eyes to the fossils buried in the earth. With his help, Marsh found many fossils of trilobites, which were prehistoric sea creatures that looked like crabs. After that experience, Marsh decided to devote himself to the science of geology, which eventually led him to pursue paleontology. He attended Yale College and then was hired there as a professor. Although he enjoyed the process of digging for fossils, his time was better spent in the lab, where he could analyze the finds, reconstruct skeletons, and write papers about his research for scientific journals. He became obsessed with naming dinosaurs, especially in naming more than his rival, another respected paleontologist named Edward Drinker Cope. Marsh ended up winning that battle. By the time he died of pneumonia in 1899, he had discovered and named 80 dinosaurs; Cope, who died two years earlier, has credit for only 56.

Paleontologist

O. C. Marsh

Hitting It on the Head

When O. C. Marsh mistakenly put a *Camarasaurus* skull on the end of an *Apatosaurus* neck—calling the "new" creature *Brontosaurus*—in 1879, he set in motion a series of mistakes that would take years to undo. In 1900, Henry Fairfield Osborn, the director of the American Museum of Natural History in New York City, followed Marsh's lead and added a cast of the *Camarasaurus* skull to the headless *Apatosaurus* at his museum. Even after Earl Douglass had found an *Apatosaurus* skeleton with a skull located nearby, Pittsburgh's Carnegie Museum of Natural History chose to put that skull in a box and store it for more than 50 years; the museum had another cast of the *Camarasaurus* skull created to use on its display instead. No one believed that the smaller, narrower skull that Douglass had found was right for such a gigantic body. Then, in 1975, paleontologists Jack McIntosh and David Berman identified the correct skull for *Apatosaurus*, prompting most museums, including the Carnegie, to change their recreations. Although scientists believe the right skull is now being used (as pictured below), no *Apatosaurus* skeleton has yet been found with its skull still attached.

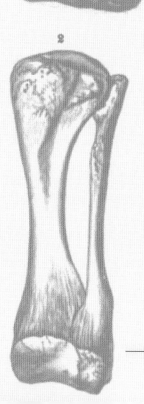

The large bones of *Apatosaurus* supported a massive amount of weight—as much as 30 tons (27 t).

had been buried, he knew that the bones most likely dated to the Late Jurassic Period (about 154 to 144 million years ago) and that the dinosaur had probably eaten the ferns and other plants that were abundant on Earth at that time. Marsh could tell by the sheer size of the bones that they supported an enormous animal that possibly weighed 20 tons (18.4 t) or more. But in his rush to name as many dinosaurs as quickly as possible, Marsh also made some mistakes. The most significant of his blunders almost cost *Apatosaurus* its name.

Because so many large skeletons were being discovered within such a short time frame—quarries in Colorado, Wyoming, and Utah were teeming with both bones and men eager to dig them out and sell the fossils for a profit—paleontologists were pressed to study the bones and give them a name. In 1879, Marsh was sent 25 crates of bones that had been unearthed in Como Bluff, Wyoming. He was so excited by the discovery that he failed to recognize that these bones, while slightly smaller, were actually identical to those of the dinosaur he had named *Apatosaurus*.

The second skeleton was more complete but smaller than the first. At nearly 50 feet (15.2 m) long, its size still eclipsed that of most other sauropods previously discovered. When a skull was found in close proximity to the rest of the bones, Marsh decided it must be a match and determined that he could now give this new giant a name. He called it *Brontosaurus*, which means "thunder lizard."

What Marsh didn't realize was that the long, rounded skull he attached to the *Brontosaurus* bones actually belonged to a *Camarasaurus* that had been buried nearby in the same quarry. Because the skull appeared to fit proportionally with the rest of the skeleton, Marsh left it attached to the creature's long neck. And because no other *Apatosaurus* skulls had been discovered (even today, only a few have been unearthed), no one else realized that it wasn't the right fit, either. Almost a century would go by before Marsh's mistake finally came to light.

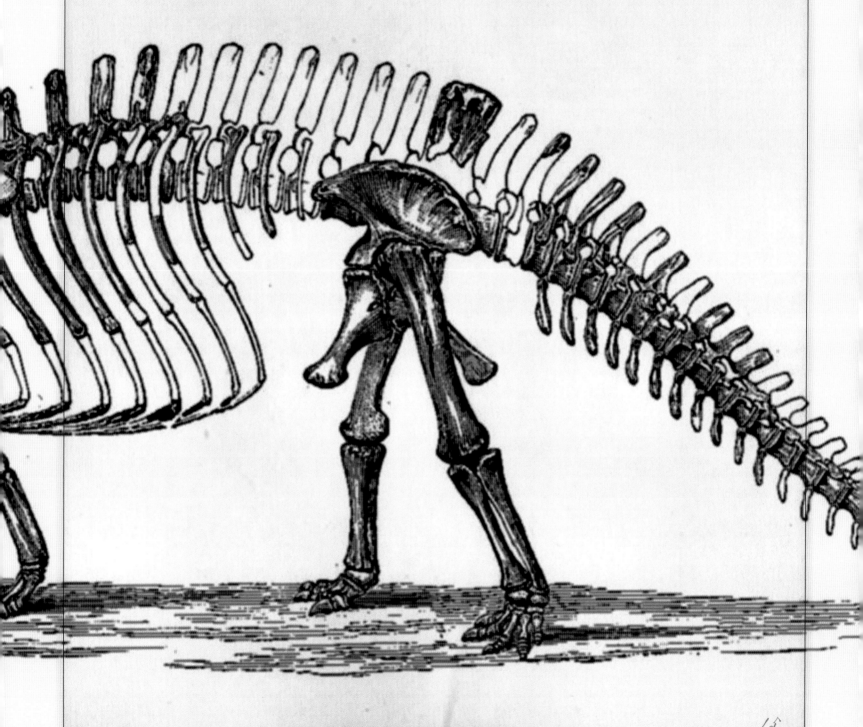

APATOSAURUS

15

It took only a few years, however, for other paleontologists to realize that Marsh's naming of the giant sauropod had been in error. In 1903, a paleontologist named Elmer Riggs was able to prove that *Brontosaurus* was in actuality an older, larger *Apatosaurus*. Marsh had assumed that the two belonged to the same family but had not accounted for the possibility that the specimens represented the same dinosaur at different stages of development. No matter what name they assigned it, paleontologists knew even then that *Apatosaurus* was likely one of the largest creatures ever to have walked on land.

Even though Elmer Riggs (below, at left) settled the naming debate, museums continued to label *Apatosaurus* specimens as "Brontosaurus" into the 1950s (opposite).

GENTLE GIANT

Although part of *Apatosaurus*'s name comes from a Greek word for "deceptive," there was nothing sneaky about the giant creature. Including its tail, it stretched between 70 and 80 feet (21–24 m) long—the length of two school buses parked one in front of the other. Its 30-ton (27 t) body weighed as much as five full-grown elephants; when it walked, it would have sounded like a herd of elephants crashing through the trees. Its enormous body was too big for it to be able to move quickly or hide easily when predators approached.

But *Apatosaurus* did not need to be stealthy to survive. Its size alone deterred many predators, most of which were a great deal smaller. Those not intimidated by *Apatosaurus*'s massive girth were often struck down by a blow from its powerful tail. That tail extended as much as 30 feet (9 m) off the back of its body and included 82 bones, and it could snap like a whip, sending such ferocious enemies as *Allosaurus* flying through the air.

If an attacker managed to get close, *Apatosaurus* could have struck at it with the large, thumblike claw that protruded from each of its front feet. It is possible that *Apatosaurus* could have even reared up on its massive hind legs, which were slightly longer than those in front, to tower threateningly

Deceptive Bones

It is possible that O. C. Marsh was trying to be clever when he named the collection of massive dinosaur bones he had been sent in 1877 "deceptive lizard." Clearly, it would have been hard for such an enormous creature to sneak around or hide in any way. But Marsh's records at Yale, where the renowned paleontologist served as the director of the Peabody Museum, suggest that he had had a different reason for choosing the name *Apatosaurus*. The "deception" in its name actually refers to its bones. In studying the first fossilized specimens that had been uncovered, Marsh noticed that the skeletal features of the dinosaur's tail were deceptively similar to those of a family of marine reptiles known as mosasaurs. That may have made distinguishing the two species from one another difficult. The name Marsh mistakenly granted to his next *Apatosaurus* find was probably more appropriate in describing the large reptile, as *Brontosaurus* means "thunder lizard." It is quite likely that each step that the dinosaur took did resonate through its surroundings like thunder.

The Late Jurassic hunter *Allosaurus* lived from about 150 to 144 million years ago and usually pursued smaller sauropods and stegosaurs rather than *Apatosaurus*.

over an adversary. Its muscular tail could have acted as a third leg to help it balance. Then, if necessary, it could have come crashing down with all the force of its weight in its two-foot-wide (0.6 m) front feet, crushing anything below it.

However, there is evidence to suggest that *Apatosaurus* was not completely immune from attack. Some of the bones that have been unearthed are marked with deep gouges from the long, razor-sharp teeth of such **carnivores** as *Allosaurus*. Scientists cannot tell from those marks whether the giant plant-eater was killed and then eaten or **scavenged** after it had died of other causes. But it

Fearsome Foe

Not many dinosaurs would try to take down a gigantic *Apatosaurus*. But even though it was less than half the size of the plant-eating sauropod, *Allosaurus* was not afraid to attack. *Allosaurus*, one of the biggest Jurassic carnivores, was built for strength, speed, and power. Its hind legs were tall and muscular, and its S-shaped neck was thick and strong. Its long tail helped it balance as it attacked, and its jaws could open upward and outward, allowing it to snag huge chunks of flesh with its sawlike teeth. Although *Allosaurus* weighed approximately 2 tons (1.8 t) and measured 35 feet (11 m) from its huge head to the tip of its tail, it was nimble enough to sneak through the dense undergrowth and jump out at its prey with its jaws wide open. Hunting in packs may have helped *Allosaurus* take down large sauropods such as *Apatosaurus*. It may have also simply targeted sick or wounded giants who were unable to fight back or flee— those who would not have lashed out their dangerous tails in defense.

is possible that a nimble *Allosaurus* could have brought down an unsuspecting *Apatosaurus*.

Apatosaurus spent much more time eating than it did fighting. Its size demanded that it eat almost continuously throughout the day in order to fuel its body and maintain its growth. It spent most of its waking hours browsing for fresh ferns on the ground, reaching up for the tasty green leaves of short, stubby **cycads**, or pulling cones off the **conifers** that were abundant at the time. It used its long, pencil-shaped teeth to tear the leaves off branches and to pull plants out of the ground—but those dull teeth did little to help the giant dinosaur chew its fibrous food. It swallowed most of its meals whole.

The dinosaur also occasionally swallowed rocks, which helped mash up the leaves, plants, and cones in its stomach. Those rocks, called gastroliths, were tossed around in its stomach along with the food. The stomach churned the food and rocks together until everything was broken up enough to be digested. But because the rocks were

heavier than the food, they settled to the bottom of *Apatosaurus*'s stomach as the food passed through the rest of its system. Paleontologists have often found smooth, round gastroliths nestled near the rib cages of *Apatosaurus* fossils.

Although it was constantly foraging for food, scientists believe that a full-grown adult *Apatosaurus* probably consumed fewer than 1,000 pounds (453 kg)

The bones nearest the base of an *Apatosaurus*'s neck were huge and got progressively smaller the farther they went toward the head.

of food per day. That figure represents only a fraction of its total body weight. But because scientists believe that dinosaurs such as *Apatosaurus* were cold-blooded, like modern **reptiles**, they didn't need to create their own warmth from the food they ate. *Apatosaurus*'s body temperature varied according to its surroundings; the sun warmed it up, while shade and chilly water cooled it down. In contrast, many modern plant-eating animals, including cows and giraffes, are warm-blooded and need to eat larger quantities of food to help their bodies produce the heat that keeps them warm.

Apatosaurus's lengthy neck also helped the dinosaur conserve energy. Instead of walking around looking for each new bite, it could swing its neck from side to side and clear a wide area of foliage before moving on to the next place. Because it could stand still for long periods of time, it needed less food to fuel its movements.

When *Apatosaurus*
was ready for a break
from its steady eating, it likely
waded into a pool of water to cool
off and drown any **parasites** that might
have attached to its thick, leathery hide.
Sometimes it would nap while standing in the water.
But paleontologists assume that, like many of the large
plant-eaters, *Apatosaurus* was a fitful sleeper. It likely dozed
only in short spurts, even at night, partly because it needed to
continue eating and partly because sleeping would have left it more
vulnerable to attacks from predators.

Although its body was enormous, *Apatosaurus* had a tiny head. Its
skull measured only about two feet (0.6 m) in length and was short
and flat instead of rounded. Its teeth took up most of the front of its
head, leaving its nostrils to sit up high between the eyes. Its brain was
also quite small; most scientists agree that it would have been about
the size of a computer mouse.

Brawniness was clearly more important than braininess to
Apatosaurus. But its big build was also a problem for the gentle giant.
It reached full size quickly in its life cycle, which may have been up to

100 years long; some scientists believe that by the time it was 12 years old, *Apatosaurus* could have reached its maximum weight of 30 tons (27 t). Although that rapid growth helped protect it from predators at a younger age, it also put a lot of stress on other bodily functions.

Its heart, for example, had to be quite large to pump blood all the way to its long extremities. The act of mating and then laying eggs would have been difficult for such an enormous dinosaur as well. And no matter how abundant plant life was during the Jurassic Period, there simply wasn't enough time in the day or room in *Apatosaurus*'s mouth for all the food it needed to continue growing.

Bringing up Babies

Although pieces of about a dozen *Apatosaurus* skeletons have been found, no fossilized eggs have yet been discovered that can be linked directly to *Apatosaurus*. Despite that missing piece of evidence, many scientists believe that, like most sauropods, *Apatosaurus* did lay eggs, and those eggs were enormous. Some sauropod eggs have been found to measure as much as one foot (30 cm) around. Those discoveries reveal another interesting fact: Because the eggs were found in a linear pattern, not clustered together in a nest, it's possible that the dinosaurs literally laid the eggs as they were walking amidst vegetation, which would have meant that *Apatosaurus* mothers, like other sauropods, did not take care of either their eggs or the baby dinosaurs once they were hatched. Some scientists contend, though, that *Apatosaurus* may have been warm-blooded and given birth to live young instead of laying eggs. That might help explain how the dinosaurs were able to grow so quickly, because they could have weighed 200 to 300 pounds (91–136 kg) as newborns. This is one of the *Apatosaurus* puzzles that paleontologists are still trying to figure out.

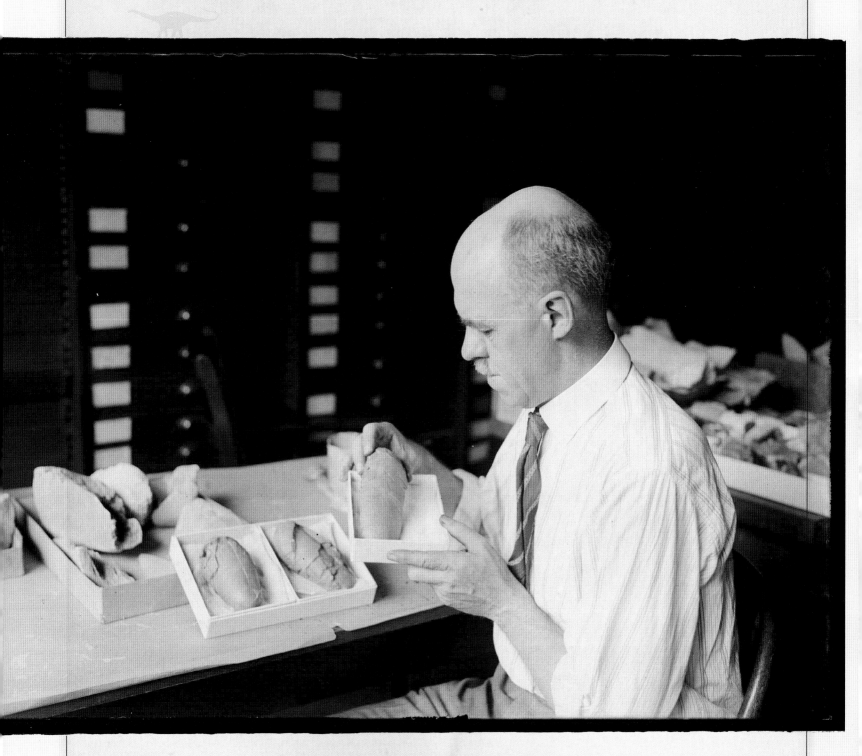

Charles W. Gilmore, a paleontologist who specialized in North American and Asian dinosaurs, made casts of eggs to replicate the originals.

Diplodocus (opposite) had a more flexible tail than its fellow sauropod *Apatosaurus* (pictured), possibly enabling the dinosaur to prop itself up.

LAND OF PLENTY

The world was ripe for the emergence of giant dinosaurs when the Jurassic Period began approximately 206 million years ago. The **climate** was becoming warmer and wetter than it had been in the previous Triassic Period, and sea levels rose, flooding low-lying plains. The combination of increased moisture and warmth created prime growing conditions for more forms of plant life. And as plants became more abundant, the creatures that ate them also became more numerous—and more enormous.

Thus, the Jurassic Period saw the rise of a group of enormous plant-eaters, from the earliest known sauropods such as *Barapasaurus* to the later-developing *Brachiosaurus*, *Diplodocus*, *Ultrasaurus*, and *Apatosaurus*. Smaller stegosaurs, including *Stegosaurus*, were also **evolving** and living off the lush plant growth. But as these peaceful plant-eaters enjoyed a more plentiful menu of ferns, cycads, conifers, and **ginkgoes**, the carnivorous predators that preyed on them thrived as well.

Allosaurus and *Ceratosaurus* became feared adversaries, growing up to 35 feet (10.5 m) in length. Although they were still significantly smaller than such 70-foot (21 m) sauropods as *Apatosaurus*, they had speed and biting strength on their side. And because their plant-eating prey would attack only if provoked, these fearsome hunters had no natural enemies.

They did, however, have other company. Reptiles had become prominent during the Triassic Period, but during the Jurassic, those animals also took flight. The flying reptiles were called pterosaurs, and they traveled through the Jurassic skies on leathery wings. By the end of the period, they were joined by another group of fliers: birds. With feathers to help them fly, birds began to diversify rapidly at the end of the Jurassic Period, and they continue to be common today.

As sea levels began to rise, so did the number of animals living in the water. Although marine reptiles, such as the paddling *Plesiosaurus*, were more common by far, the first fishlike predators also started to appear—including sharks, whose earliest ancestors had existed for millions of years by then. Cephalopods began evolving into early ancestors of the squids and octopuses that lurk in today's oceans. Tiny land **mammals** were also beginning to evolve, but these were still mouselike both in size and behavior; most would flit through the foliage and seek food and water only at night, when the risk of being trampled by an enormous foot or snapped up between powerful jaws was much lower.

Dinosaurs were undeniably the dominant **species** on land. But which dinosaurs ruled over which areas was becoming much more defined. As the Jurassic Period began, the supercontinent of Pangaea, which contained almost all of Earth's landmasses, was in

The long-necked *Plesiosaurus* (below) swam in the seas, while *Brachiosaurus* (opposite) was the tallest land-dwelling creature of the Late Jurassic.

Dinosaur National Monument

On October 4, 1915, president Woodrow Wilson officially declared an 80-acre (32 ha) section of land in Colorado and Utah as Dinosaur National Monument. The area was full of fossils, including *Apatosaurus* bones. Earl Douglass, who worked for Pittsburgh's Carnegie Museum of Natural History, had found an *Apatosaurus* fossil there in 1909. As Douglass and other bone hunters continued to work in the sandstone ledges of the area, they found even more dinosaur bones. They named the site the Carnegie Quarry, because most of the fossils found there were sent to the Carnegie Museum in Pittsburgh. But as more people found out about the potential richness of the site, the museum became worried that valuable scientific research could be lost if amateurs started digging in the quarry. So museum officials **lobbied** the U.S. Department of the Interior to protect the area and were relieved when President Wilson decided to preserve the land. Today, a dinosaur museum at the site, which now includes more than 200,000 acres (80,937 ha) of land, is open to the public. Museums and universities can still conduct research there as well.

the process of breaking into sections—a southern landmass known as Gondwana and a northern fragment called Laurasia. As the period progressed, those large sections also began to break up and drift apart into more distinct continents separated by the earliest version of the Atlantic Ocean.

North America was also becoming more clearly separated from South America, which meant that the dinosaurs living on each continent began growing apart as well. Although fossils of Jurassic sauropods have been found on both continents, the dinosaurs that wandered the plains of North America—including *Apatosaurus*—did not meander into South America. The specimens that have been found on each continent are distinct from one another. South America was home to such enormous plant-eaters as *Amargasaurus* and *Argentinosaurus* and to huge carnivores such as the aptly named *Giganotosaurus*—none of which have yet been found anywhere in North America.

    Apatosaurus, meanwhile, roamed throughout the western part of what is now the United States during the later years of the Jurassic Period. Some scientists speculate that it may have even existed in Europe, although fossils of its bones have not yet been found there. So far, its remains have been extracted only from the states of Colorado, Utah, Oklahoma, and Wyoming.

    Fossilized footprints of many Jurassic sauropods, including *Apatosaurus*, suggest that they lived in herds and traveled together

Archaeological digs (opposite) uncover clues to Earth's past during times when the continents were in different positions and configurations.

in search of food. As they grew physically bigger, and as their numbers increased as well, finding enough food to satisfy their endless hunger became more and more difficult—even in the lush era in which they lived. Even a small herd of *Apatosaurus* could quickly consume all of the vegetation availa ble in a large area.

That constant grazing posed another problem for the creatures. It took a great deal of energy to move their bodies over short distances, let alone when they had to cover a matter of miles in search of fresh food. The more they were forced to wander, the more they would have needed to eat in order to keep up the pace. It would have been easy for their food supply to become strained quite quickly.

It is also possible that, as it evolved into ever larger forms, *Apatosaurus*'s massive body could have become too unwieldy. To support a body growing to 30 tons (27 t) and beyond, the amount of bone mass would have needed to increase proportionately, and more muscles would have been needed to move those large bones.

Eventually,
Apatosaurus and
the other enormous
dinosaurs of its
time might have
grown too big for their own good.
Although no one knows for sure why
Apatosaurus became **extinct** at the end of the Late
Jurassic, about 144 million years ago, scientists believe
that such size-related complications could have contributed
to its demise. The cause may never be known. But by the
time the Cretaceous Period began, the gentle *Apatosaurus* giants
were no longer rumbling across the earth.

UNDERSTANDING *APATOSAURUS*

From its initial discovery in 1877, paleontologists knew that *Apatosaurus* was an enormous animal. Long before the first full skeleton was finally assembled in 1975, when the first intact *Apatosaurus* skull was recovered, scientists were able to make certain assumptions based on the size of the bones that had been found, including vertebrae that were more than three feet (0.9 m) around. Most of those assumptions have turned out to be quite close to the mark.

But as scientists find more fossils and analyze them with more sophisticated methods and modern equipment, the more they understand about *Apatosaurus*. Today they realize that some of the behaviors that early paleontologists ascribed to *Apatosaurus* likely weren't possible. One example is the reach of *Apatosaurus*'s neck. For many years, it was assumed that the dinosaur used its long neck to reach the tops of trees, much like modern giraffes do. Early pictures of *Apatosaurus* almost always show it holding its head high and stretching up above its body for leaves. Most museums displayed *Apatosaurus* skeletons with their long necks stretched out toward the ceiling, as everyone assumed that it was able to lift its head 25 to 30 feet (7.6–9 m) straight into the air.

Now most scientists believe that *Apatosaurus* held its head straight out from its body most of the time. It certainly was able to lift it, but it probably was able to attain an elevation of only 16 feet (4.8 m) above

Artist Francis Phillipps showed a more anatomically correct *Apatosaurus* by not extending the neck and head much higher than the shoulders.

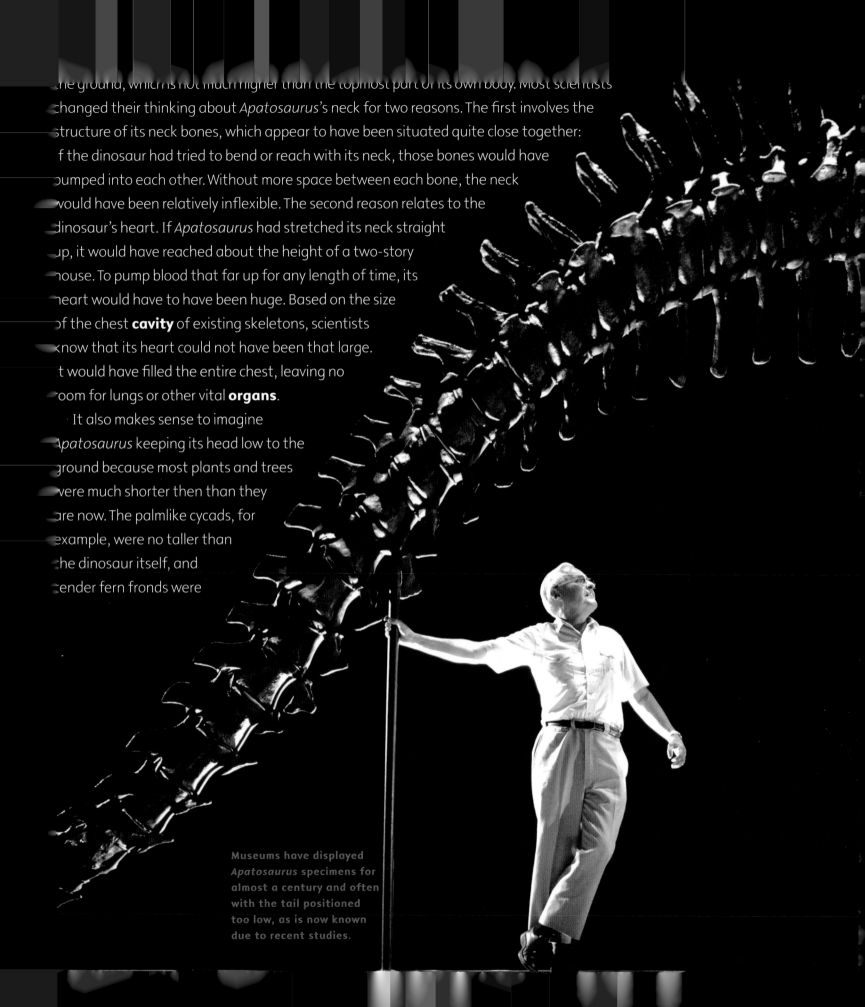

the ground, which is not much higher than the topmost part of its own body. Most scientists changed their thinking about *Apatosaurus*'s neck for two reasons. The first involves the structure of its neck bones, which appear to have been situated quite close together: If the dinosaur had tried to bend or reach with its neck, those bones would have bumped into each other. Without more space between each bone, the neck would have been relatively inflexible. The second reason relates to the dinosaur's heart. If *Apatosaurus* had stretched its neck straight up, it would have reached about the height of a two-story house. To pump blood that far up for any length of time, its heart would have to have been huge. Based on the size of the chest **cavity** of existing skeletons, scientists know that its heart could not have been that large. It would have filled the entire chest, leaving no room for lungs or other vital **organs**.

It also makes sense to imagine *Apatosaurus* keeping its head low to the ground because most plants and trees were much shorter then than they are now. The palmlike cycads, for example, were no taller than the dinosaur itself, and tender fern fronds were

Museums have displayed *Apatosaurus* specimens for almost a century and often with the tail positioned too low, as is now known due to recent studies.

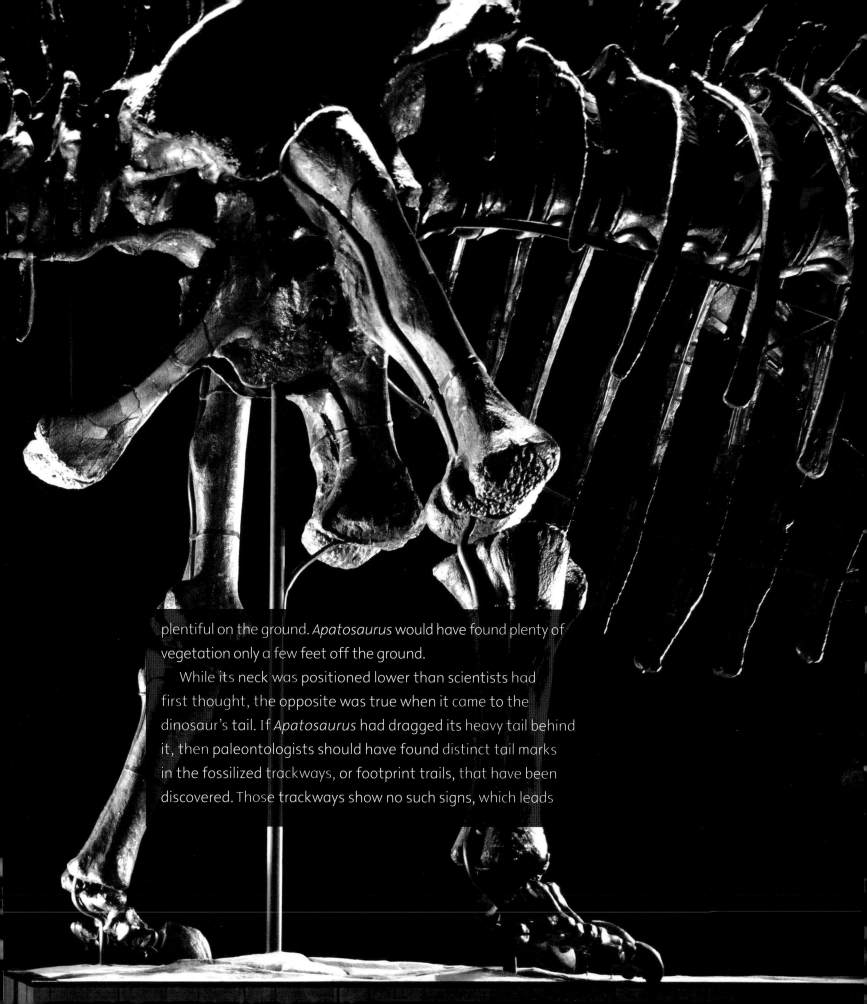

plentiful on the ground. *Apatosaurus* would have found plenty of vegetation only a few feet off the ground.

While its neck was positioned lower than scientists had first thought, the opposite was true when it came to the dinosaur's tail. If *Apatosaurus* had dragged its heavy tail behind it, then paleontologists should have found distinct tail marks in the fossilized trackways, or footprint trails, that have been discovered. Those trackways show no such signs, which leads

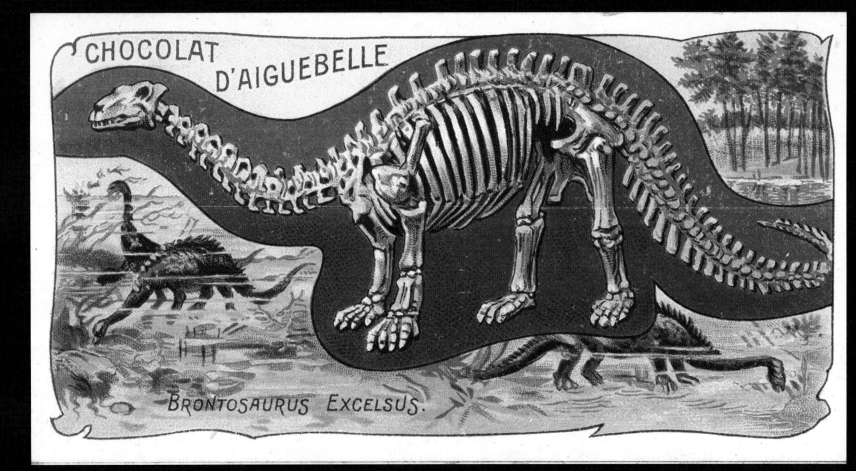

CHOCOLAT D'AIGUEBELLE

BRONTOSAURUS EXCELSUS.

Maintaining a Mistake

Although the scientific community has long accepted that the name *Apatosaurus* should be used in place of *Brontosaurus*, the general public has had more difficulty in adjusting to that change. Many people know the long-necked dinosaur only by the name *Brontosaurus*, which was given to an *Apatosaurus* skeleton in error in 1879. The continued confusion has been perpetuated by popular culture, especially in the movies. Both the original 1933 version of *King Kong* and the 2005 remake include *Brontosaurus* references. Also, one of the main characters in the children's film *The Land Before Time* is a young *Brontosaurus* named Littlefoot. The United States Postal Service (USPS) even knowingly opted to use the more popular name instead of the scientifically correct name when it released a series of four dinosaur stamps in 1989. That decision, along with the fact that the flying pterosaur *Pteranodon* was misspelled as "Pteradon" (and technically isn't even a dinosaur), brought outrage from paleontologists. The USPS defended itself by saying that even though *Brontosaurus* was not the correct name, it was "more familiar to the general population." It apologized only for the spelling mistake.

scientists to believe that *Apatosaurus* held its tail up off the ground as it walked.

Keeping the tail elevated could have been a protective measure. If sauropods did live in herds, as scientists suspect, then there would have been a large number of enormous dinosaurs in close proximity to each other at all times. It would have been common for those dinosaurs to accidentally step on each other's tails as they maneuvered through the forest looking for food. It also would have been easy for hungry carnivores to chomp down on the meaty tail when no one was looking. Holding the tail up helped *Apatosaurus* control what happened to it.

How it was positioned was not the only confusion that swirled around *Apatosaurus*'s tail. When the first few skeletons were found in the late 1800s, paleontologists did their best to identify which bones belonged to which dinosaurs. But occasionally, mistakes were made—as with the *Camarasaurus* skull that O. C. Marsh unknowingly attached to an *Apatosaurus* body, leading to a new name and a mistaken identity. In 1883, a similar mistake was made with the tail of the first reconstructed *Apatosaurus* skeleton. In place of the 82-bone, 30-foot (9 m) tail that should have been mounted with the *Apatosaurus* body, a much shorter tail was used. That tail, like the skull Marsh put on its head, actually belonged to a *Camarasaurus.*

That mistake was much easier to resolve than the misplaced skull because it didn't take as long for bone hunters to unearth a complete *Apatosaurus* tail. Locating an intact skull, which was much more fragile and often shattered into small pieces, was far more complicated. It wasn't until 1975 that two American paleontologists, Jack McIntosh and David Berman, realized that the skull on Marsh's original *Brontosaurus* skeleton was that of a *Camarasaurus*. A shorter skull had been found that belonged to *Apatosaurus*, and they could tell that it truly fit on what had been called *Brontosaurus*'s body.

Although that discovery officially resolved the *Apatosaurus/Brontosaurus* name controversy, it did not result in a change on the nameplate at the Yale Peabody Museum's Great Hall of Dinosaurs. The skeleton that Marsh named *Brontosaurus* in 1879 was mounted and displayed there, where it remains to this day with a sign in front of the

Andrew Carnegie (below) made many smart investments over the course of his life, especially in the field of scientific advancement.

The Carnegie Connection

Andrew Carnegie had a dream: The wealthy businessman and generous philanthropist wanted to bring dinosaur bones to his home city of Pittsburgh, Pennsylvania, and have their skeletons be the main attraction at the Carnegie Museum of Natural History, which was named in his honor. So he sent several bone hunters to search for fossils in Wyoming, Utah, and Colorado—including a talented young paleontologist named Earl Douglass. In 1909, Douglass found a remarkable specimen to bring back to Carnegie: an almost complete *Apatosaurus* skeleton. That skeleton was mounted and displayed at the original Carnegie Museum as *Apatosaurus louisae*, in honor of Carnegie's wife, Louise.

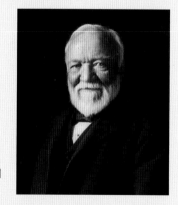

Today, it is part of the impressive "Dinosaurs in Their Time" exhibit at the Carnegie Museum of Natural History, one of four Carnegie museums in Pittsburgh. The exhibit also includes a baby *Apatosaurus* skeleton that has been part of the museum's collection for more than 100 years and a pair of *Tyrannosaurus rex* skeletons locked in battle. *Apatosaurus louisae* and most of the other skeletons were taken apart and remounted in more scientifically correct poses in 2007, following the results of recent research.

43.

G Caselli.

skeleton that reads "Brontosaurus"—but in quotation marks and not italics, as most dinosaur names are written, in recognition of the fact that it is not an official scientific name.

Scientists continue to study dinosaur bones, including *Apatosaurus* fossils, in hopes of learning more about the animals' existence and their extinction. Even today, professional paleontologists and amateur fossil hunters alike still delight in the discovery of a new bone or fossil. Despite the many technological advances that have come about in the years since Marsh and Cope's endeavors, removing and restoring dinosaur bones remains a time-consuming and labor-intensive process.

For many scientists, young and old, the work is worth the results. Any time they learn something new about *Apatosaurus* or another dinosaur, they come closer to understanding what life on Earth was like millions of years ago. More than a century after the first *Apatosaurus* bones were discovered, scientists are still learning more about them and their reptilian relatives. And a century from now, they will probably have still more to discover.

Apatosaurus compared with a five-foot-tall (152 cm) human

46

GLOSSARY

carnivores—animals that feed on other animals

cavity—a naturally hollow place within the body

climate—the long-term weather conditions of an area

conifers—evergreen trees, such as pines and firs, that bear cones

cycads—tropical palmlike plants that bear large cones

evolving—adapting or changing over time to survive in a certain environment

extinct—having no living members

geological—pertaining to the science of the rocks and other physical structures of the earth

ginkgoes—large ornamental trees with fan-shaped leaves, fleshy fruit, and edible nuts

herbivorous—describing an animal that feeds only on plants

lobbied—sought to persuade or influence a person on an issue

mammals—warm-blooded animals that have a backbone and hair or fur, give birth to live young, and produce milk to feed their young

organs—parts of the body adapted to perform specific functions

paleontologist—a scientist who studies fossilized plants and animals

parasites—animals or plants that live on or inside another living thing (called a host) while giving nothing back to the host; some parasites cause disease or even death

reptiles—cold-blooded animals with scaly skin that typically lay eggs on land

scavenged—to have gathered and eaten the rotting flesh of animals found dead

sediment—crushed, rocky matter that settles to the bottom of a liquid, such as a body of water

species—a group of living organisms that share similar characteristics and can mate with one another

SELECTED BIBLIOGRAPHY

Barrett, Paul. *National Geographic Dinosaurs*. Washington, D.C.: National Geographic Society, 2001.

Burnie, David. *The Kingfisher Illustrated Dinosaur Encyclopedia*. New York: Kingfisher Publications, 2001.

Colbert, Edwin H. *The Great Dinosaur Hunters and Their Discoveries*. New York: Dover Publications, 1984.

Farlow, James O., and M. K. Brett-Surman. *The Complete Dinosaur*. Bloomington, Ind.: Indiana University Press, 1997.

Kimmel, Elizabeth Cody. *Dinosaur Bone War: Cope and Marsh's Fossil Feud*. New York: Random House Books for Young Readers, 2006.

Parker, Steve. *Dinosaurus: The Complete Guide to Dinosaurs*. Buffalo, N.Y.: Firefly Books, 2003.

INDEX

READ MORE

Currie, Philip J., and Michael Tropea. *Dinosaur Imagery: The Science of Lost Worlds and Jurassic Art*. San Diego, Calif.: Academic Press, 2000.

Lansky, Kathryn. *Dinosaur Dig*. New York: Morrow Junior Books, 1990.

Ottaviani, Jim. *Bone Sharps, Cowboys, and Thunder Lizards*. Ann Arbor, Mich.: G-T Labs, 2005.

Schomp, Virginia. *Apatosaurus and Other Giant Long-Necked Plant-Eaters*. Tarrytown, N.Y.: Marshall Cavendish Children, 2002.